Don't Hop with Pop!

Anders Hanson

Consulting Editor, Diane Craig, M.A./Reading Specialist

ABDO
Publishing Company

Published by ABDO Publishing Company, 4940 Viking Drive, Edina, Minnesota 55435.

Printed in the United States.

Credits
Edited by: Pam Price
Curriculum Coordinator: Nancy Tuminelly
Cover and Interior Design and Production: Mighty Media
Photo Credits: AbleStock, Rubberball Productions

Library of Congress Cataloging-in-Publication Data

Hanson, Anders, 1980-
    Don't hop with pop! / Anders Hanson.
        p. cm. -- (First rhymes)
    Includes index.
    ISBN 1-59679-471-2 (hardcover)
    ISBN 1-59679-472-0 (paperback)
        1. English language--Rhyme--Juvenile literature. I. Title. II. Series.
PE1517.H364 2005
808.1--dc22

                                                                    2005049156

SandCastle™ books are created by a professional team of educators, reading specialists, and content developers around five essential components that include phonemic awareness, phonics, vocabulary, text comprehension, and fluency. All books are written, reviewed, and leveled for guided reading and early intervention reading, and designed for use in shared, guided, and independent reading and writing activities to support a balanced approach to literacy instruction.

Let Us Know

After reading the book, SandCastle would like you to tell us your stories about reading. What is your favorite page? Was there something hard that you needed help with? Share the ups and downs of learning to read. We want to hear from you! To get posted on the ABDO Publishing Company Web site, send us e-mail at:

sandcastle@abdopub.com

SandCastle Level: Beginning

drop

hop

mop

pop

shop

See them .

He can .

We look at the .

We like the .

I see a .

The stars drop.

Ken likes to hop.

I mop the floor.

The pop is cold.

The shop is open.

A clumsy clown
walks into a shop.

He asks the
man in the shop
for a soda pop.

The clown in the shop
does a little hop
when he gets his pop.

But as he does his hop,
the clown lets his pop
drop on the floor
of the shop.

If the clown did not hop,
the pop would not drop.

Now he has to mop
up the shop.

About SandCastle™

A professional team of educators, reading specialists, and content developers created the SandCastle™ series to support young readers as they develop reading skills and strategies and increase their general knowledge. The SandCastle™ series has four levels that correspond to early literacy development in young children. The levels are provided to help teachers and parents select the appropriate books for young readers.

Emerging Readers
(no flags)

Beginning Readers
(1 flag)

Transitional Readers
(2 flags)

Fluent Readers
(3 flags)

These levels are meant only as a guide. All levels are subject to change.

To see a complete list of SandCastle™ books and other nonfiction titles from ABDO Publishing Company, visit **www.abdopub.com** or contact us at:
4940 Viking Drive, Edina, Minnesota 55435 • 1-800-800-1312 • fax: 1-952-831-1632